MW00444036

The Heart That Grew Three Sizes
Children's Leader Guide

The Heart That Grew Three Sizes:
Finding Faith in the Story of the Grinch

The Heart That Grew Three Sizes
978-1-7910-1732-3
978-1-7910-1733-0 eBook

The Heart That Grew Three Sizes: Leader Guide
978-1-7910-1734-7
978-1-7910-1735-4 eBook

The Heart That Grew Three Sizes: DVD
978-1-7910-1736-1

The Heart That Grew Three Sizes: Youth Study Book
978-1-7910-1741-5
978-1-7910-1742-2 eBook

The Heart That Grew Three Sizes: Children's Leader Guide
978-1-7910-1745-3

The Heart That Grew Three Sizes: Worship Resources
978-1-7910-1743-9 Flash Drive
978-1-7910-1744-6 Download

Also by Matt Rawle

The Faith of a Mockingbird
The Salvation of Doctor Who
Hollywood Jesus
The Redemption of Scrooge
What Makes a Hero?
The Gift of the Nutcracker
The Grace of Les Miserables

With Magrey R. deVega, Ingrid McIntyre, and April Casperson

Almost Christmas

For more information, visit MattRawle.com.

MATT RAWLE

THE HEART THAT GREW THREE SIZES

CHILDREN'S LEADER GUIDE

by Erin Floyd

FINDING FAITH IN THE STORY OF THE GRINCH

Abingdon Press / Nashville

The Heart That Grew Three Sizes:
Finding Faith in the Story of the Grinch
Children's Leader Guide

Copyright © 2021 Abingdon Press
All rights reserved.

No part of this work may be reproduced or transmitted in any form or by any means, electronic or mechanical, including photocopying and recording, or by any information storage or retrieval system, except as may be expressly permitted by the 1976 Copyright Act, the 1998 Digital Millennium Copyright Act, or in writing from the publisher. Requests for permission can be addressed to Rights and Permissions, The United Methodist Publishing House, 2222 Rosa L. Parks Blvd., Nashville, TN 37228-1306 or e-mailed to permissions@abingdonpress.com.

Local churches that have purchased this book may photocopy the pages within the book specifically labeled as "reproducible" for use with the lessons as indicated, provided each copy retains the copyright notice printed thereon:

Copyright © 2021 Abingdon Press
Permission is granted to photocopy this page for local church use only.

ISBN-13: 978-1-7910-1745-3

Scripture quotations are taken from the Common English Bible, copyright 2011. Used by permission. All rights reserved.

21 22 23 24 25 26 27 28 29 30 — 10 9 8 7 6 5 4 3 2 1
MANUFACTURED IN THE UNITED STATES OF AMERICA

Table of Contents

Introduction

This children's leader guide is designed for use with Matt Rawle's book *The Heart That Grew Three Sizes: Finding Faith in the Story of the Grinch*. Rawle's book explores the familiar Christmas story, *How the Grinch Stole Christmas!* and ways the Grinch's transformation and redemption point us to aspects of the Christian faith, especially the hope we find in Jesus's birth. This guide includes four lessons for children during the Advent season, that draw on both the biblical stories of Jesus's birth and the story of the Grinch. Children will follow these lessons throughout the liturgical season of Advent as they prepare to welcome baby Jesus into the world on Christmas.

The lessons in this guide, designed for children in kindergarten through the sixth grade, are presented in a large group/small group format. Children begin with time spent at activity centers, followed by time together as a large group. Next, children will move into age-specific groups, where they will spend the remainder of their class time. Each lesson plan contains the following sections:

Focus for the Teacher

The information in this section will provide you with background information about the week's lesson. Use this section as a devotional as you prepare to lead this session.

Explore Interest Groups

This section provides three activities that invite children to explore the theme for the day. These activities offer an introduction to the Bible story. You may choose to offer all of the activities for children to choose from or pick your favorite based on your group's specific needs.

Large Group

The large group time introduces the Bible story that points toward Christmas. Children will engage with the Bible story and Advent theme through hands-on experiences and songs. Large group time will also include learning a memory verse. Encourage the children to practice their Bible skills by helping the children find passages in the Bible, even if the activity does not require reading directly from the Bible.

Small Groups

Small groups offer age-specific opportunities to explore the Advent theme of the day and the Bible story. It is recommended that each small group contain no more than ten children. You may need to have more than one group for each age level. The small group time will provide opportunities to read and discuss the day's Bible story as well as a portion of *How the Grinch Stole Christmas!*

Younger Children
The activities in this section are designed for children in grades K–2.

Older Children
The activities in this section are designed for children in grades 3–6.

Reproducible Pages

At the end of each lesson are reproducible pages, to be photocopied and handed out for all the children to use during that lesson's activities or to be used as a guide for the teacher.

Schedule

Many churches have weeknight programs that include an evening meal; an intergenerational gathering time; and classes for children, youth, and adults. The following schedule illustrates one way to organize a weeknight program.

Weeknight

5:00	Meal
6:00	Intergenerational gathering introducing weekly themes and places for the lesson. This time may include presentations, skits, music, and opening or closing prayers.
6:15–7:15	Classes for children, youth, and adults.

Churches may want to do this study as a Sunday school program. This setting would be similar to the weeknight setting. The following schedule takes into account a shorter class time, which is the norm for Sunday morning programs.

Sunday

10 minutes	Intergenerational gathering
45 minutes	Classes for children, youth, and adults

Choose a schedule that works best for your congregation and its existing Christian education programs.

May God richly bless your fellowship as you lead children in these sessions and provide opportunities for them to encounter the God who comes to be with us, transform us, and redeem us.

1 When Everything Is Wrong

Objectives

The children will

- hear the story of the angel appearing to Mary.
- learn about the joy of Jesus.
- explore what it means to be joyful.

Bible Story

Luke 1:26-56

Bible Verse

"Happy is she who believed that the Lord would fulfill the promises he made to her."

(Luke 1:45)

Focus for the Teacher

How the Grinch Stole Christmas! is a familiar Christmas story. We read, watch, and tell the story of a mean, green Grinch, who tried to ruin Christmas. The Grinch *hated* Christmas.

On the other hand, our Bible story is about Mary and the birth of Jesus. Although the angel's announcement brought Mary much confusion and fear, Mary finds joy.

Children might wonder how the Grinch could hate Christmas. For many children, Christmas is a magical time of year filled with joy. Joy is what the Christmas season is all about. But the Grinch does not understand this quite yet. First the Grinch must go on a journey in which he discovers Christmas means more than what he thought. It's a journey toward joy.

Sometimes joy is not our first response to wonderful news. When Mary hears the news from the angel, she is worried and concerned. Joy does not always begin with big smiles or ecstatic jumping; sometimes joy takes time.

In today's lesson, you can help children join you on a journey toward the joy of Christmas. This journey, which takes place during Advent, is our movement toward the joy of Christmas. With Mary as our guide, together we can welcome the joyous news of the coming of Christ Jesus.

Explore Interest Groups

Be sure that adult leaders are waiting when the first child arrives. Greet and welcome each child. Get the child involved in one of the activities below that interests him or her and introduces the theme for the day's activities.

Jesus Is Joy

- Give each child a copy of **Reproducible 1a: Jesus Is Joy.**

- **SAY:** Today we are learning about joy.

- **ASK:** What does joy look like? feel like? Did Jesus's mother Mary feel joy when Jesus was born?

- **SAY:** Jesus brought Mary joy, and Jesus brings each of us joy.

- Have the children color and decorate **Reproducible 1a: Jesus Is Joy.**

- Have or help the children cut out the heart. Then glue the heart on cardstock.

- Punch a hole through the top of the heart. Then tie string or ribbon through the hole to make an ornament.

- Send home the Jesus Is Joy ornament.

- **SAY:** You can hang your ornament on your Christmas tree or somewhere in your home to remember the joy Jesus brings us at Christmas.

Prepare

- ✓ Provide cardstock, paper punch, string or ribbon, and coloring utensils.

- ✓ Make copies of **Reproducible 1a: Jesus Is Joy.**

A Story of Joy

- **SAY:** Today we will hear the Bible story about an angel giving a message to Mary.

- Give each child a copy of **Reproducible 1b: A Story of Joy.**

- Have the children form pairs and fill in the blanks of their Story of Joy mad-lib. One child should ask the other for a word to fill in each blank, write it down, and then read the story aloud once all the blanks are filled in. Then the children should switch.

- Invite the children to share their stories with the group.

Prepare

- ✓ Provide pencils.

- ✓ Make copies of **Reproducible 1b: A Story of Joy.**

Prepare

✓ Provide wrapping paper, gift bags, tissue paper, ribbon, and other gift-wrapping supplies.

✓ Provide scissors and markers.

Gifts of Joy

- **SAY:** Today we hear about the gift of Jesus.

- **ASK:** Do you like getting gifts? Do you like giving gifts? What is the best gift you have ever received? How do you feel when you receive a gift?

- Show the children the wrapping supplies.

- Invite the children to make a gift from the supplies. Encourage the children to be creative.

- **SAY:** Jesus is a gift of joy. When we give gifts, we are giving joy to others.

Large Group

Joy Journey

- Gather the children in a line.

- Give each child a musical instrument.

- **SAY:** Today, we learn about the announcement of Jesus's birth. An angel appears to Mary to tell her this joyous news.

- **ASK:** How do you think Mary felt? How would you feel if an angel appeared to you?

- **SAY:** During Christmas we wait four weeks for Jesus. This story is just the beginning of our joy journey. Let's go on a journey to share the joyous news that Jesus is coming.

- Hand out the instruments

- Lead the children around your church space as they play instruments.

- You can also invite the children to sing familiar Christmas hymns/carols.

- Return to the gathering space and collect the instruments.

- **ASK:** How does it feel to spread joy?

Shout for Joy

- Read today's Bible verse. "Happy is she who believed that the Lord would fulfill the promises he made to her" (Luke 1:45).

- **SAY:** Today's Bible verse is a reminder of the joy Jesus brings to us on Christmas.

- **ASK:** What things make you joyful? How do you know if someone is feeling happy or joyful?

- Divide the children into three groups. Assign each group a part of the Bible verse.
  - o Happy is she who believed
  - o that the Lord would fulfill
  - o the promises he made to her.

- Point to each group several times and encourage the children to chant the assigned part of the Bible verse.

Prepare
- ✓ Provide musical instruments such as tambourines, maracas, triangles, and ukuleles.
- ✓ Inform other gathering groups that the children will be having a musical procession. Invite others to join.

When Everything Is Wrong

Share the News

- **SAY:** In today's Bible story, an angel appears to Mary to tell her good news. The angel tells Mary that Jesus is coming. I want you to think about good news you want to share.

- Divide the children into small groups (no more than five in a group).

- Pick one child in each group to start. When you say go, have the first child whisper to the child to the right, good news that he or she wishes to share. Have the children pass the good news around the circle until it reaches the last child.

- When the last child receives the good news, the child stands up and shouts the good news. The first child must confirm that what she or he heard was correct. If not, the group must start again.

- Play the game until a group shouts each child's good news.

Small Groups

Divide the children into small groups. You may organize the groups around age levels or around readers and nonreaders. Keep the groups small, with a maximum of ten children in each group. You may need to have more than one group of each age level.

Younger Children

- Gather the children together. Read the Bible story: Luke 1:26-56.

- After reading the Bible story, read pages 1–5 of *How the Grinch Stole Christmas!* Start with, "Every Who," through, "for tomorrow, he knew...."

- **ASK:** Who was in our Bible story today? How did Mary feel? Who was in our second story? How did the Grinch feel? How does Christmas make you feel?

- Give each child a copy of **Reproducible 1c: Joy Maze**.

- Have the children complete the maze. When the children are finished, let them color the maze.

- **SAY:** Sometimes we feel angry or sad, but the birth of Jesus brings us great joy.

- *TIP:* The Bible story uses the words *virgin* and *sexual relations*. Consider reading the story from a Storybook Bible.

Prepare

- ✓ Provide Bibles and a copy of *How the Grinch Stole Christmas!*

- ✓ Photocopy **Reproducible 1c: Joy Maze.**

Prepare

✓ Provide blank paper and writing utensils.

✓ Provide Bibles and a copy of *How the Grinch Stole Christmas!*

Older Children

- Gather the children together. Select a volunteer to read the Bible story: Luke 1:26-56.

- After reading the Bible story, read pages 1–5 of *How the Grinch Stole Christmas!* Start with, "Every Who," through, "for tomorrow, he knew....."

- **SAY:** Today we heard a story about Mary and another one about the Grinch.

- **ASK:** What was your favorite part of the stories?

- Give each child a piece of paper and a writing utensil.

- Have the children draw two overlapping circles on the paper like a Venn Diagram.

- Have the children write *Mary* at the top of the right circle and *The Grinch* at the top of the left circle.

- Invite the children to write down facts about the stories of Mary and the Grinch. In the middle of the circle, the children will write any similarities.

- Invite willing volunteers to share what they discovered.

- **ASK:** Was there joy in each story? How did each story begin? What do you think will happen next in our stories?

- **SAY:** Sometimes things happen, and it is hard to see or find joy.

- **ASK:** Do you always feel joyful? Why or why not?

- **SAY:** Sometimes it is hard to find joy in difficult situations. But, on Christmas Jesus is born, and he brings joy to the whole world.

- Sing the hymn "Joyful, Joyful, We Adore Thee" (*The United Methodist Hymnal*, 89).

The Heart That Grew Three Sizes: Children's Leader Guide

Jesus Is Joy

Copyright © 2021 Abingdon Press • *Permission is granted to photocopy this page for local church use only.*

A Story of Joy

When the angel came to _____, God said to

(name)

"_____ The Lord is with you!" _____ was

(action word) (name)

_____ by these words and wondered what kind of

(emotion)

greeting this might be. The angel said, "_____.

(a phrase)

God is honoring you. Look! You will have a _____,

(person or thing)

and you will name him Jesus. He will be _____

(describing word)

and he will be called _____. The Lord God will give

(second name)

him _____. He will rule over _____ forever,

(thing) (place)

and there will be no end to his kingdom."

Copyright © 2021 Abingdon Press • *Permission is granted to photocopy this page for local church use only.*

Joy Maze

Copyright © 2021 Abingdon Press • *Permission is granted to photocopy this page for local church use only.*

You can pick which activities you want to do!

2 When Christmas Isn't Christmas

Objectives

The children will

- hear the story of the magi following the star.
- experience joy.
- know Jesus brings joy.

Bible Story

Matthew 2:1-15

Bible Verse

When they saw the star, they were filled with joy. (Matthew 2:10)

Focus for the Teacher

We are continuing a journey toward joy. We begin by going on a journey with the magi. The Bible story tells us about the magi following a star to find the baby Jesus. The journey was long, and it is likely Jesus was a toddler when they finally arrived. However, when the magi found the child, they were filled with joy.

In the lesson, we will also read more about the Grinch. In the next section of our story, we have the Who village excitedly preparing for Christmas. They are buying toys, making noise, hanging stockings, and spreading joy. This bothered the Grinch. He did not want to share in the Christmas joy. So, the Grinch made a plan to ruin Christmas.

The magi, the Whos, and the Grinch are all leading us on a journey toward Christmas. All the characters in our stories are preparing for Christmas in different ways. When reading these stories, children can see that our journey toward celebrating the birth of Jesus can look different for everyone. Sometimes it takes time to find joy at Christmas. As you guide children through this lesson, allow the children to acknowledge how they experience the Christmas season. Then remind the children, that the joy of Christmas is coming.

Explore Interest Groups

Be sure that adult leaders are waiting when the first child arrives. Greet and welcome each child. Get the child involved in one of the activities below that interests him or her and introduces the theme for the day's activities.

Glow Dough

- Divide the children into three groups. Have the children put on the plastic gloves.

- Give each group one part of the dough and one of the food colorings.

- Have each group follow the directions on **Reproducible 2a: Glow Dough** to mix the food coloring into their dough.

- Once the groups are finished coloring their dough, bring the groups back together. Have the children roll and swirl the three parts of dough together. Have the children make sure each color of dough is visible.

- Then, add the glitter and stars.

- Divide the Glow Dough into plastic bags, one for each child.

- Send home the dough.

Prepare

✓ Gather the supplies listed on **Reproducible 2a: Glow Dough.**

✓ Follow the directions on **Reproducible 2a: Glow Dough** to prepare the dough mixture ahead of time.

Optional Activity

Sandy Stars

- Lay out the sand trays with the glow sticks.

- Turn out the lights and light the glow sticks (help younger children light the sticks if needed).

- Invite the children to use the glow sticks like a toothpick to move the sand around. Have the children write the word *joy* or draw a star in the sand or create a different word or image that expresses joy.

- As the children are interacting with the sand, have them say a prayer.

- **PRAY:** God of the stars, thank you for bringing us the joy of Jesus. Amen.

Prepare

✓ Provide small trays or shallow bottom plastic containers.

✓ Place sand in the trays.

✓ Provide glow sticks.

Optional Activity

Prepare

✓ Provide scissors, crayons, markers, colored pencils, cotton stuffing or other soft material, string or yarn, paper punches.

✓ Make copies of **Reproducible 2c: Star Pillows** (enough for two copies for each child).

Star Pillows

- Give each child two copies of **Reproducible 2c: Star Pillows.**

- Let the children color and decorate the stars, then cut out the stars.

- Lead them to punch holes on the marked spots. Place the two stars on top of each other. Align the holes.

- Show the children how to string the yarn through the holes. Before stringing the stars fully together, direct them to place the stuffing inside the stars. When the stars are fully strung together, tie off the yarn. Cut off excess yarn.

Large Group

Bring all the children together to experience the Bible story.

Gold Star

- Divide the children into pairs. Encourage an older child to work with a younger child.

- Give each pair a copy of **Reproducible 2b: Gold Star**, a writing utensil, and one sheet of gold star stickers.

- **SAY:** This week, we continue our journey toward joy.

- **ASK:** Who knows what we will find at the end of our journey? How do you feel while you wait for the birth of baby Jesus?

- Have the children walk around the room in pairs to find a friend who matches each description in the box. When they find a matching friend, place a gold star in the box.

- Continue the activity as long as time allows. Then, gather the children together.

- **ASK:** What did you learn about your friends?

Prepare

✓ Provide gold star stickers and writing utensils.

✓ Make copies of **Reproducible 2b: Gold Star.**

Prepare

✓ Provide heavyweight construction paper or cardstock, a star pattern, a circle pattern, scissors, markers, glue, and craft sticks.

I Am Joyful

- Give each child a piece of paper.

- Invite the children to use the star pattern to trace a star on the paper.

- Then, have the children use a marker to draw a circle with the circle pattern in the middle of the star. The circle should be as big as the child's face.

- Have the children cut out the middle of the circle and the star shape. Then let the children color and decorate the star.

- Glue a craft stick to the bottom of the star.

- Invite the children to practice holding the star stick in front of their face so their face is in the hole in the star.

- Once all the children have completed their stars, gather the children together.

- Have the children place the star over their face.

- Have them repeat a chant after you.
  - o Shout, shout, shout to the stars!
  - o Jesus is on his way.
  - o Jesus bring joy for everyone.
  - o Let's all share our joy today!

- Have the children find a friend and share something that brings them joy.

- Repeat the chant again.

- Do this as long as time allows.

Small Groups

Divide the children into small groups. You may organize the groups around age levels or around readers and nonreaders. Keep the groups small, with a maximum of ten children in each group. You may need to have more than one group of each age level.

Younger Children

- Gather the children together. Read the Bible story: Matthew 2:1-15.

- After reading the Bible story, read pages 6–10 of *How the Grinch Stole Christmas!* Start with, "all the Who girls and boys," through, "I must stop this Christmas from coming!…But HOW?".

- **SAY:** The magi went on a journey to find baby Jesus.

- **ASK:** How did the magi find Jesus? Why were they looking for him?

- **SAY:** We also read about the Whos getting ready for Christmas.

- **ASK:** What were the Whos doing to prepare for Christmas? How do you think they felt as they prepared?

- **SAY:** Both of our stories help us on our journey toward Christmas joy! Let's use a special star to remind us of our journey.

- Give each child a star.

- **SAY:** This is a special star. It is our joy star. It can help us remember the joy Jesus brings.

- Turn off the lights. Let the children notice how the stars glow.

- **SAY:** No matter what, even in the darkness and in the light, God gives us light and joy through the birth of Jesus. You can keep this star to remember the star that led the magi to Jesus and the joy Jesus brings.

- Let the children take home the stars.

Prepare

✓ Provide Bibles and a copy of *How the Grinch Stole Christmas!*

✓ Provide glow-in-the-dark stars. Place the glow stars in bright light before the lesson. With permanent markers, write on each star the word *Joy.*

Prepare

✓ Provide Bibles and a copy of *How the Grinch Stole Christmas!*

✓ Provide clay, googly eyes, toothpicks, buttons, and chenille stems.

Older Children

- Gather the children together. Select a volunteer to read the Bible story: Matthew 2:1-15.

- After reading the Bible story, read pages 6–10 of *How the Grinch Stole Christmas!* Start with, "all the Who girls and boys," through, "I must stop this Christmas from coming!…But HOW?".

- **ASK:** What do you think the Grinch is going to do next? Why do you think the Grinch is angry? Have you ever been angry? What feelings do you have about Christmas?

- **ASK:** What do you think the magi were feeling about Jesus? Why did they look for him? What do you think they did after they went home?

- Show the children the supplies. Invite the children to use the supplies to create a character emotion.

- Encourage the children to be creative with the supplies to make figures or facial expressions. Then have the children come up with a name for their emotion.

- Invite willing volunteers to share.

- **PRAY:** Dear God, thank you for being there no matter what I am feeling, and thank you for bringing Jesus to give us joy at Christmas. Amen.

Glow Dough

Ingredients

3 cups flour

3 cups water

1½ cups salt

3 tbsp. vegetable oil

3 tsp. cream of tartar

Food coloring blue, purple, turquoise

Glitter (optional)

Tiny gold craft stars

Plastic bags

Plastic gloves

This recipe makes about enough for four children. Increase the recipe as needed for the size of the group you expect.

Directions

Prepare Ahead

Mix the flour, water, salt, vegetable oil, and cream of tartar together. Then cook the ingredients over medium heat until mixture thickens. Once the dough is thick, divide the dough into three pieces.

In the class, tell the children to:

- Put on plastic gloves. Use the food coloring to dye each piece of dough a different color. Use your hands to mix the color into the dough.

- Next, mix each color of the dough together so it looks swirled. Try not to overmix.

- If you choose, add glitter and stars to the dough.

Copyright © 2021 Abingdon Press • *Permission is granted to photocopy this page for local church use only.*

Reproducible 2b

Gold Star

Find someone who . . .	
Loves Christmas! Ask why.	
Has a family member coming to visit for Christmas. Ask who.	
Is traveling for Christmas. Ask where.	
Does not like waiting for Christmas. Ask why.	
Eats a special meal for Christmas. Ask what.	
Has decorated their Christmas tree. Ask when.	
Has gone caroling. Ask if it was fun.	
Has a telescope. Ask how to use it.	
Is excited to get a gift for Christmas. Ask what it is.	
Has bought a gift for someone else for Christmas. Ask when they are giving the gift.	
Has read *How the Grinch Stole Christmas!* Ask about their favorite part.	

Copyright © 2021 Abingdon Press • *Permission is granted to photocopy this page for local church use only.*

Star Pillows

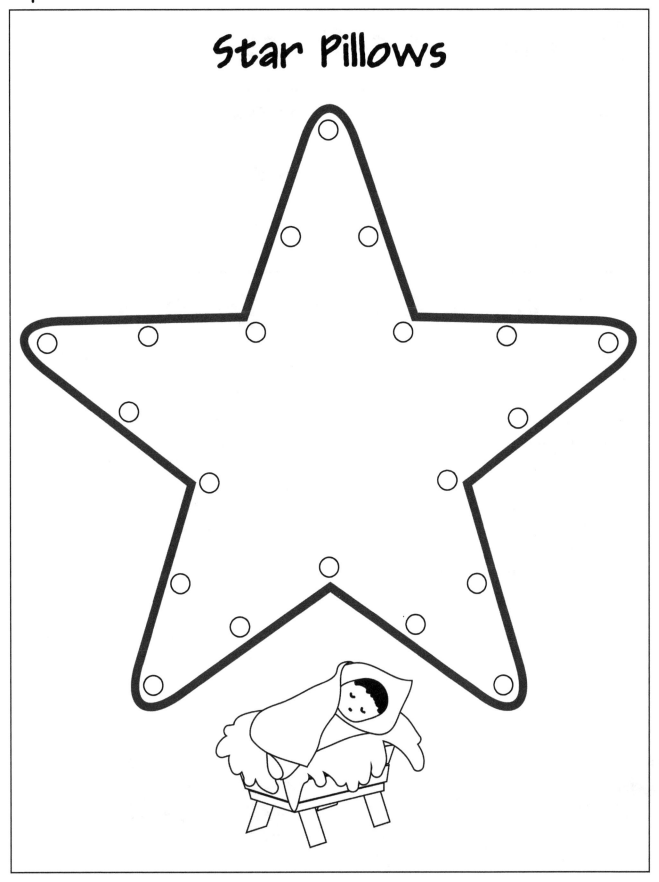

Copyright © 2021 Abingdon Press • *Permission is granted to photocopy this page for local church use only.*

3 When Light Shines

Objectives

The children will

- hear the story about the light of Christ.

- learn about Jesus's light shining for each of us.

- explore how Jesus represents light.

Bible Story

John 1:1-14

Bible Verse

The true light that shines on all people was coming into the world. (John 1:9)

Focus for the Teacher

Today we learn about light. In the Bible story, we hear about Jesus, the light of the world. Jesus comes, and though unrecognized, he shines through darkness and brings great joy and great light. We also experience the continued journey of the Grinch. The angry, mean Grinch is plowing through Whoville to destroy Christmas. But little do we know—the Grinch will soon be surrounded by joy and light.

The Grinch might be our darkness in this story. But darkness is not always a bad thing. When it is dark, we must adjust our eyes to see. The Scripture says, "The light shines in the darkness, / and the darkness doesn't extinguish the light" (John 1:5). There is much to be seen, even when it is dark.

The Bible teaching is a reminder that although there is darkness, in Jesus we find the light. Jesus does not remove darkness, but rather shows up in the darkness. In *The Heart That Grew Three Sizes*, author Matt Rawle notes that when the Grinch notices Cindy Lou Who, "she asks why the Grinch is taking the tree away. Without so much as a blink, the Grinch says that the lights on one side of the tree aren't working, and he's taking the tree to his workshop where he will fix it up. I don't think it's an accident that the Grinch calls attention to lights not working."

Soon the light will shine, and morning will come. With new light comes the birth of a brand-new baby. A baby that will fix all broken lights. This is the joy of Christmas. The light is coming to repair what was once broken. Jesus will shine light in our darkness. And when the light shines, we rejoice, because he brings light to the whole world.

Explore Interest Groups

Be sure that adult leaders are waiting when the first child arrives. Greet and welcome each child. Get the child involved in one of the activities below that interests him or her and introduces the theme for the day's activities.

Sunlight Sticker

- Give each child a copy of **Reproducible 3a: Sunlight Christmas Lights.**

- Have the children color and cut out the Christmas light outline and then trace the outline onto the non-adhesive side of the contact paper.

- Glue the tissue squares inside the Christmas light shape on the contact paper outline.

- Once the glue has dried, remove the backing of the contact paper, and stick it to the plastic binder sheet.

- Cut out the Christmas light outline.

- Punch a hole at the top of the Christmas light and string together.

- Hang up the children's Christmas lights in a window, so that the sun shines through the tissue paper.

The Light of the World

- **ASK:** What would the world be like without light? Where does light come from? How does Jesus represent light?

- Give each child one binder clip, one craft stick, one battery, one LED light, one short foil strip, one long foil strip, tape, and scissors.

- Have the children tape the long foil strip to the back, bottom side of the craft stick and the short strip to the front, top side of the craft stick. Be sure that the foil strips do not touch each other.

- Have the children clip a medium-size binder clip to their craft stick. On the bottom, the metal prong should touch the foil. On the top, the prong should be raised and no part of the metal should touch the foil.

- Have the children place the coin cell battery on the top of their craft stick, on the foil, with the + side facing down. Place the battery far enough from the binder clip so the prong of the clip will touch the battery when they lower the prong down.

Prepare

- ✓ Provide colored tissue paper, scissors, contact paper, glue sticks, clear plastic binder sheets, hole punch, and string.

- ✓ Photocopy **Reproducible 3a: Sunlight Christmas Lights.**

- ✓ Cut or tear tissue paper into small squares.

Prepare

- ✓ Provide binder clips, jumbo craft sticks, 3 V coin cell batteries (CR 2032), LED lights, aluminum foil, transparent tape, scissors.

- ✓ Cut the aluminum foil into half-inch wide strips. Cut some strips the length of the craft sticks and some half the length of the craft sticks. Each child will need one short strip and one long strip.

- Help the children tape the battery in place (over the top side only) using clear tape.

- Have the children take their LED light and gently spread the two wires (leads) apart.

- Tape the longer lead to the top of the craft stick and the shorter lead to the bottom side of the craft stick so that both wires are touching the foil.

- When the prong is lowered to the battery, it should complete the circuit and cause the light to come on. Experiment with creating light. Lift and lower the metal prong of your binder clip to turn your LED light on and off.

- **SAY:** Now we have light. The binder clip acts as a switch to create light. Jesus also gives us light. Jesus is the light for the whole world.

Prepare

✓ Provide one large canvas, squirt bottles (one per color), tablespoons, corn starch, warm water, neon paints, a black light flashlight.

✓ Locate **Reproducible 3b: Glow Paint.**

✓ Add the corn starch to the squirt bottles before class.

Glowing Paint

- Help the children follow the directions on **Reproducible 3b: Glow Paint** to create the paint.

- After making the paint, gather the children around one large, blank canvas. Allow each child, one at a time, to make designs on the canvas using the paint.

- **ASK:** What do you think the colors on our canvas will look like in daylight?

- After the paint dries, use a black light to look at the children's painting.

- **SAY:** What changed when we used the black light to look at our painting? How does light help us see in the darkness?

Large Group

Light Me Up

- Pick one child to be IT. Give IT the flashlight.
- Turn off the lights and turn on the flashlight. When you say go, the children will move quickly around the room.
- If IT shines the flashlight on another child, that child is frozen.
- As children are becoming frozen, flicker the lights to unfreeze the children.
- Do this several times, then pick a new child to be IT.
- Play the game as long as time allows.

Prepare

✓ Provide a flashlight.

Stop, Slow, Glow

- Give each child a glow stick and help them activate the sticks so they glow. Have the children spread out.
- Explain what Stop, Slow, Glow means:
  - o Stop: Freeze
  - o Slow: Dance in slow motion
  - o Glow: Dance party!
- Turn off the lights.
- Say the words, *Stop, Slow, Glow*, repeating them and interchanging them, giving the children time to respond each time.
- Play the game as long as time allows.

Prepare

✓ Provide glow sticks.

Small Groups

Divide the children into small groups. You may organize the groups around age levels or around readers and nonreaders. Keep the groups small, with a maximum of ten children in each group. You may need to have more than one group of each age level.

Prepare

✓ Provide Bibles and a copy of *How the Grinch Stole Christmas!*

Younger Children

- Gather the children together. Read the Bible story: John 1:1-14.

- After reading the Bible story, read pages 11–32 of *How the Grinch Stole Christmas.* Start with, "Then he got an idea!" through, "For the other Who's mouses!"

- **ASK:** What did the Grinch do in the story? How did the Grinch feel? Why do you think the Grinch said the light was missing on one side of the tree?

- **SAY:** In our Bible story we learn about Jesus representing light.

- **ASK:** What kinds of things shine like a light?

- **SAY:** Jesus's joy brings us happiness so we can be bright lights for others. This means we share joy with the whole world. Just like Jesus.

- Sing "This Little Light of Mine."

- Have the children hold up one finger to represent the light.
  o This little light of mine, I'm goin'a let it shine,
    this little light of mine, I'm goin'a let it shine;
    this little light of mine, I'm goin'a let it shine,
    let it shine, let it shine, let it shine.
  o Everywhere I go, I'm goin'a let it shine,
    everywhere I go, I'm goin'a let it shine;
    everywhere I go, I'm goin'a let it shine,
    let it shine, let it shine, let it shine.

(*The United Methodist Hymnal*, 585. Adapt. © The United Methodist Publishing House)

The Heart That Grew Three Sizes: Children's Leader Guide

Older Children

- Gather the children together. Select a volunteer to read the Bible story: John 1:1-14.

- After reading the Bible story, read pages 11–32 of *How the Grinch Stole Christmas*. Start with, "Then he got an idea!" through "For the other Who's mouses!"

- **ASK:** What part of the Bible passage stood out to you? What part of the Grinch's story stood out to you? What might have happened if the Grinch tried to ruin Christmas during the day instead of at night?

- Read today's Bible verse.
  - o The true light that shines on all people
       was coming into the world. (John 1:9)

- **ASK:** What does it mean that light is coming for the whole world?

- Turn off the lights. Have the children close their eyes. Help the children calm their bodies by breathing in and out.

- Lead the children in the following breath prayer.
  - o Breathe in—Jesus is the light.
       Breathe out—Light shines all around me.

- Do this several times.

Prepare

✓ Provide Bibles and a copy of *How the Grinch Stole Christmas!*

Glow Paint

Supplies:

Squirt bottles

Tablespoons

Cornstarch

Warm water

Neon paints

A black light flashlight

Paper towels or wet wipes

Instructions:

1. Fill the squirt bottles one-third full with cornstarch, using one squirt bottle for each color of chalk you wish to make. *If you wish to make your paint thicker, add more cornstarch.*

2. Add 1 tablespoon of neon paint to each bottle.

3. Fill the bottles with very warm water and stir.

4. Then, secure the lids on the bottles and shake them vigorously until all of the ingredients are combined.

Copyright © 2021 Abingdon Press • *Permission is granted to photocopy this page for local church use only.*

4 When Joy Is Our Song

Objectives

The children will

- hear the story of the birth of Jesus.
- learn about making a joyful noise.
- explore joy through music.

Bible Story

Luke 2:1-20

Bible Verse

The angel said, "Don't be afraid! Look! I bring good news to you—wonderful, joyous news for all people." (Luke 2:10)

Focus for the Teacher

After we have journeyed toward joy, we discover the Grinch has decided to ruin Christmas. Whoville awakens to stolen presents and torn down Christmas trees. It should have been, the Grinch thought, anything but joyous. However, despite the missing decorations and no gifts under the tree, the Whos begin to sing.

The song annoys the Grinch. How could the Whos possibly be singing? But they sang. They sang loud enough that the Grinch could hear their raised communal voices. There was one thing that could not be taken, and that was the Whos' joy.

In the familiar biblical Christmas story, we also find great joy. The joyous news of Jesus's birth is proclaimed, and a Savior is born. We have been waiting for this moment, and just maybe the Grinch had been waiting too. His heart grew three sizes when he heard the Whos' song and realized that Christmas was more than he thought, and it surely grew more when he joined the Whos at their table to celebrate Christmas. The Grinch, all of Whoville, and each of us have found our joy. So let us sing. Joy to the world!

Explore Interest Groups

Be sure that adult leaders are waiting when the first child arrives. Greet and welcome each child. Get the child involved in one of the activities below that interests him or her and introduces the theme for the day's activities.

Joy Song

- **SAY:** Today we sing for joy. Jesus is born!

- **ASK:** What brings you joy? How do you feel on Christmas?

- **SAY:** Do you have a favorite song? How does music make you feel?

- Play the joyful music and invite the children to listen to the words. Then have the children write their own song about joy or draw pictures of someone singing a joyful song.

- Let willing volunteers share their song or picture.

Prepare

- ✓ Provide paper and writing utensils.

- ✓ A computer or CD player, playing joyful hymns such as, "Joyful, Joyful, We Adore Thee," "Joy to the World," or others that you may choose.

Make Music

- Have the children place the straws on top of the cardboard in order, right to the left from the tallest to the shortest, to make a musical instrument played by blowing through the straws. (The cardboard should be about one inch from the end of all the straws.)

- Use duct tape and place over and around the straws to hold the cardboard and straws together.

- Let the children use the instrument to play music.

Prepare

- ✓ Cut eight large circumference straws: 9, 8, 7, 6⅜, 5¾, 5, 4½, 4¼ inches long.

- ✓ Supply duct tape.

- ✓ Cut a piece of cardboard two inches wide and long enough to fit all of the straws side-by-side.

Spread Joy   *Megaphones*

- **SAY:** Today we have great joy. Jesus is born!

- **ASK:** What joyful message do you want to share today?

- Invite the children to use the directions on **Reproducible 4b: Spread Joy** to create a megaphone.

- Let the children take turns using their megaphones to share joyful news.

Prepare

- ✓ Provide scissors, glue, and coloring utensils.

- ✓ Photocopy: **Reproducible 4b: Spread Joy.**

Large Group

Prepare

✓ Provide chalk or tape.

✓ Go outside and recreate the hopscotch sample **Reproducible 4a: Jump for Joy** or use tape to make it inside.

Prepare

✓ Find and print an image of baby Jesus or the word *Joy*.

Jump for Joy

- Have the children line up.

- One at a time, have each child follow the hopscotch.

- When they reach the square that says "JOY," the children must jump up and down for ten seconds and shout for joy.

- Allow the children to follow the hopscotch several times.

Find the Joy

- Divide the children into two groups. Give one group the picture of baby Jesus or the word *Joy*.

- Direct group one to close their eyes or leave the room. Have group two pick one person to hide the picture. Have the chosen child share with group two where she or he chose to hide the picture.

- When the picture is hidden, invite group one to open their eyes or come back in the room.

- As a group, group one must go around the space and look for the picture.

- If the group is getting close, group two must sing songs louder and louder. If the group is moving away from the picture, group two should sing softer.

- Do this until group one finds the picture.

- Then switch the groups.

Small Groups

Divide the children into small groups. You may organize the groups around age levels or around readers and nonreaders. Keep the groups small, with a maximum of ten children in each group. You may need to have more than one group of each age level.

Younger Children

- Gather the children together. Read the Bible story: Luke 2:1-20.

- After reading the Bible story, read pages 33–43 of *How the Grinch Stole Christmas!* Start with, "It was a quarter past dawn…," through, "carved the roast beast!"

- **ASK:** What happened to the shepherds? What happened to the Grinch? What did the Whos do?

- **ASK:** What surprising things happened in our Bible story? What surprising things happened in the story of the Grinch?

- **SAY:** There is a lot of surprising things in our stories today. It is amazing what joy can do!

- **ASK:** Where did you see joy in our stories today? Do you think the Grinch found joy?

- Sing "Joy to the World" (*The United Methodist Hymnal*, 246).

- Let the children use their instruments and megaphones while they sing.

  o   Joy to the world, the Lord is come!
  Let earth receive her King;
  let every heart prepare him room,
  and heaven and nature sing,
  and heaven and nature sing,
  and heaven, and heaven, and nature sing.

(*The United Methodist Hymnal*, 246 © The United Methodist Publishing House)

Prepare

- ✓ Provide Bibles and a copy of *How the Grinch Stole Christmas!*

Prepare

✓ Provide Bibles and a copy of *How the Grinch Stole Christmas!*

Older Children

- Gather the children together. Read the Bible story: Luke 2:1-20.

- After reading the Bible story, read pages 33–43 of *How the Grinch Stole Christmas!* Start with, "It was a quarter past dawn…," through, "carved the roast beast!"

- **ASK:** What happened to the shepherds? What happened to the Grinch? What did the Whos do?

- **ASK:** What surprising things happened in our Bible story? What surprising things happened in the story of the Grinch?

- **SAY:** There are a lot of surprising things in our stories today. It is amazing what joy can do!

- **ASK:** Where did you see joy in our stories today? Do you think the Grinch found joy?

- Sing "Joy to the World" (*The United Methodist Hymnal,* 246).

- Let the children use their instruments and megaphones while they sing.

  o Joy to the world, the Lord is come!
     Let earth receive her King;
     let every heart prepare him room,
     and heaven and nature sing,
     and heaven and nature sing,
     and heaven, and heaven, and nature sing.

(*The United Methodist Hymnal,* 246 © The United Methodist Publishing House)

Jump for Joy

	10	
7	8	9
	JOY	
3	4	5
	JOY	

Copyright © 2021 Abingdon Press • *Permission is granted to photocopy this page for local church use only.*

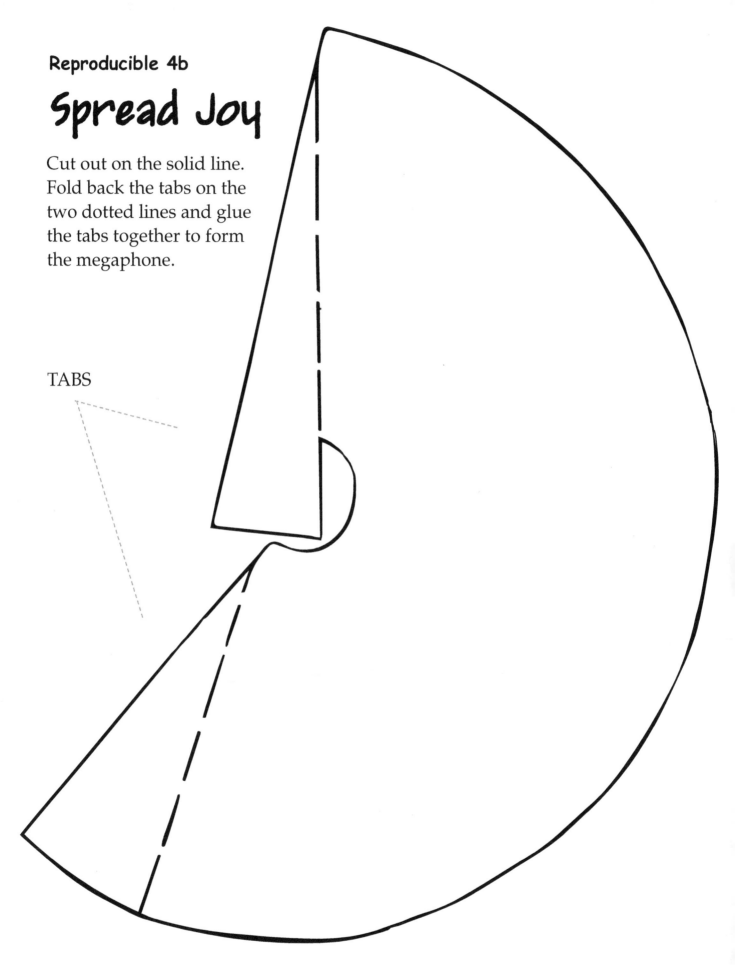

Reproducible 4b

Spread Joy

Cut out on the solid line.
Fold back the tabs on the
two dotted lines and glue
the tabs together to form
the megaphone.

TABS

Copyright © 2021 Abingdon Press • *Permission is granted to photocopy this page for local church use only.*

Bonus Coloring Pages

THE HEART
THAT GREW THREE SIZES

FINDING FAITH IN
THE STORY OF THE GRINCH

Copyright © 2021 Abingdon Press • *Permission is granted to photocopy this page for local church use only.*

Reproducible Bonus Coloring Page

Copyright © 2021 Abingdon Press • *Permission is granted to photocopy this page for local church use only.*

Copyright © 2021 Abingdon Press • *Permission is granted to photocopy this page for local church use only.*

Christ Is Born

Copyright © 2021 Abingdon Press • *Permission is granted to photocopy this page for local church use only.*

Jesus Brings Joy

Copyright © 2021 Abingdon Press • *Permission is granted to photocopy this page for local church use only.*

"The light shines in the darkness,

and the darkness doesn't extinguish the light." — (John 1:5)

Copyright © 2021 Abingdon Press • *Permission is granted to photocopy this page for local church use only.*

Joy to the World

Copyright © 2021 Abingdon Press • *Permission is granted to photocopy this page for local church use only.*

CPSIA information can be obtained
at www.ICGtesting.com
Printed in the USA
LVHW101123230921
698515LV00005B/31

9 781791 017453